Speed-A-Way

A NEW GAME FOR BOYS AND GIRLS

Editor

MARJORIE S. LARSEN

1754 Middlefield

Stockton 4, California

REVISED EDITION

BURGESS PUBLISHING COMPANY

426 South Sixth Street — Minneapolis 15, Minnesota

APPRECIATION

The originator of this game expresses her sincere appreciation to all those who have been willing to introduce Speed-a-way at their schools, clinics, and conventions; to Voit Rubber Corporation and Burgess Publishing Company for their advertising and assistance; to Carol Hooper and the girls of Redlands High School, Redlands, California, for their co-operation in making the Speed-a-way film; to Frances Carter, Marjorie Auster, and Yolanda Klaskin for their encouragement and helpfulness; to Ruth Sevy, Louise Appel, Ardelle Carlson, Marjorie Fish, Ellen Isenberg, Hermine Davidson, and her staff for their suggestions for improvement of the rules; to the original Speed-a-way committee of Loretta Stallings, Thelma Lagerberg, Dorothy Holtberg Marshall, and Kathryn Maloy, who has spend many countless hours in assisting with the revision of this guide book; to my father and mother, Mr. and Mrs. Wm. Larsen, who made it possible for the first guide to be published.

TABLE OF CONTENTS

INTRODUCTION

It was the desire to find a game that could serve as a lead-up for field hockey and the desire to find a game that could bring enjoyment and satisfaction to participants without their having to spend a great deal of time in learning complicated rules or complicated techniques that caused Speed-a-way to be formulated. Speed-a-way came into being as a new combination game--a combination of soccer, basketball, speedball, field ball, and hockey, with an opportunity for players to run with the ball. The rules of these games have served as a basis for Speed-a-way.

Speed-a-way was in the experimental stage for ten years before the first rule book was published in 1950. Girls' physical education classes at Edison High School, Stockton, California, helped to formulate the first rules. Discussions were held with students regarding various phases of the game, and suggestions were made that would make the game more fun and easier to play. In the spring of 1950, Speed-a-way was taught in other schools for the first time. With suggestions from staff members of Modesto and Oakdale High Schools, both located in California, Speed-a-way rules were clarified and were ready for publication in December, 1950.

It is not easy to get a new game introduced; one encounters many problems. But with the wonderful co-operation of physical education teachers throughout the United States, this new game was introduced at clinics and at conventions and professional publications. In 1952 a film was made which also helped in the presentation of the game. And now, ten years later, we find that Speed-a-way is being played throughout the United States, and that it has been introduced in Canada, England, India, Alaska, and Hawaii. Although Speed-a-way was originated as a game for girls, it has also found a place in the boys' physical education programs.

Speed-a-way has been a favorite with those who try it. Partipants do not have to spend a great deal of time in learning the rules or in learning the game. Speed-a-way can be adapted to almost any situation; the game is adaptable to the elementary level and is an excellent game for the junior high school level for boys and girls. High school and college students also find it enjoyable. In playing the game, a player experiences a great deal of enjoyment; there is the opportunity for vigorous activity, competition and team co-operation.

It is hoped that this revised edition of the Speed-a-way guide will clarify the rules and eliminate questions which have arisen in the original publication. Teachers from various sections of the United States have sent in suggestions and criticisms. Some of the articles in the original guide have been kept; others have been deleted or changed; new ones have been added; the rules have been revised and clarified--all we hope will make your teaching of the game easier.

Introduce Speed-a-way into your program to find just how much enjoyment players do get from participation.

Marjorie S. Larsen

ABOUT THE CONTRIBUTORS

THELMA LAGERBERG graduated in physical education from Chico State College, Chico, California. She formerly was a member of the Girls' Physical Education Department, Oakdale Union High School.

LORETTA M. STALLINGS is now on the staff of the George Washington University, Washington, D.C. She received her Bachelor's degree from Stanford University and her Masters Degree from the College of Pacific. She taught in several high schools in California.

KATHRYN MALOY is an instructor in girls' physical education at Oakdale Union High School, Oakdale, California. She received her A.B. degree from College of the Holy Names, Oakland, California and has taken graduate work at the University of California.

SUSIE MAH was formerly an Edison High School student, Stockton, California, who has shown much talent in using her artistic ability to interpret rules of various games.

LOIS FISCUS was formerly an art teacher at Edison High School, Stockton, California. She graduated from the California School of Fine Arts in Berkeley, California.

JOYCE MALONE is a member of the Girls' Physical Education Department, Edison High School, Stockton, California. She received her A.B. degree from San Jose State College and her Masters degree from the College of Pacific.

MARJORIE S. LARSEN, originator of the game of Speed-a-way, is Chairman of the Girls' Physical Education Department, Edison High School, Stockton, California. She graduated from the University of California and received her Masters degree from the College of Pacific.

WHY PLAY SPEED-A-WAY

By Thelma Lagerberg

There are many reasons why Speed-a-way is a good game to play; it offers opportunities for girls and boys with all ranges of skills to participate actively in the game and to derive pleasure from it. It may be played by a non-skilled group, who will have lots of fun because they can make progress even with the simplest methods. This does not place the game as one for lower skilled groups exclusively; those who have acquired skills can find many challenges in Speed-a-way. Speed-a-way is a game in which a wide variety of techniques and team plays can be used.

The skills used in Speed-a-way are many and varied, depending on on the group playing:

a. Fundamentally, running is one of the basic skills involved with any group; therefore, the class or teams should be physically fit and in condition for this activity.

b. Many methods of kicking the ball are used: (1) dribbling the ball with the feet can be developed to a very fine skill; (2) the running kick is frequently used to advantage; (3) the place-kick is used during active playing time and on free kicks and out-of-bounds plays; (4) the punt is often used by the backfield players, especially the goal keeper whose privilege of picking up any ball gives her many chances to punt it to her forward line; (5) the drop-kick can be used as a method of advancing the ball or as a special method of scoring which the players enjoy immensely; (6) the last specific skills involving feet and ball are stopping or trapping the ball and taking it from this stationary position and lofting it to oneself or a teammate so that it can be played as an aerial ball.

Once the ball has become an aerial ball, it may be advanced by various types of passes--one hand, two hand, underhand, overhead, chest, hook, or whatever pass is effective in a given situation.

In addition to individual and couple skills a great deal of teamwork can be developed on both ground and aerial plays, and on combinations of these. Even fullbacks can play a vital part in scoring--their long pass or punt down the field to a wing (who is not restricted by offside rules) may be run or passed over the end line for a touchdown. Because of the speed with which the ball progresses up and down the field, everyone on the team plays a very active part. The game tends to be more offensive than defensive so that the idea of the backfield following the forward line down the field is emphasized. This does not mean defensive play is eliminated--close guarding, as on throw-ins near the end line, can be stressed. The players will learn that they can't all play the ball or keep up with it (because of the speed of passes and kicks); thus the value of position play can be realized.

One may wonder at the value of another field game when we have soccer, speedball, field ball, football, hockey and such established games. We do not promote Speed-a-way as a successor to these games, but as a supplement; it is an entirely new game with distinctive features that merit its establishment in sports programs. Compared with these other sports, it offers several features.

Speed-a-way, we feel, is more adaptable to young and non-skilled groups than soccer. Soccer, in order for players to get the satisfaction of scoring, calls for skilled handling of the ball with the feet and body blocking of the ball. Beginners at field ball games lack this skill and can become discouraged. We have found Speed-a-way adapts to elementary groups because kicked ball can be caught, and even caught on the first bounce--skills learned earlier in kick ball. This allows more chance of advancing the ball to a scoring position--a vital factor in maintaining the interest of beginners. Soccer is a fine game, after more body skill is acquired, but for the first field game, we recommend Speed-a-way.

As compared to speedball, we feel Speed-a-way allows more leniency in play. If a player is not in position to catch a kicked ball, he is allowed the option of catching it on the first bounce which gives more opportunity for creating serial balls, for passing or running with the ball.

Running with the ball and the touch-tag allows for the natural desire to "take off" with the ball to score a sensational running touchdown. With girls this play answers the annual question, "Why can't we play football?" Here they get the thrill of a running, passing, or combination play with few of the dangers of football involved. This fulfillment of the desire to play football is often all the justification needed for playing the game.

Speed-a-way is an inexpensive game, especially in comparison with hockey, yet it acquaints players with positions similar to hockey, with the corner play and much team play of similar nature to that of hockey. It can serve in place of hockey or as a lead-up sport if hockey is available. For lesser skilled groups Speed-a-way is not complicated by the addition of an accessory; it involves only players and ball.

The ball handling, agility of body control and physical stamina developed during Speed-a-way season will serve their part when you move indoors for basketball. We feared our basketball players might have increased their tendency to travel, but court limitations and the idea of shooting for a goal seemed to erase their previous privilege of traveling with the ball; consequently, we had no problem there.

We could continue on the merits of Speed-a-way as we see it. We still enjoy our other team field games, but we feel Speed-a-way deserves to be right up there in our program. It is less technical as far as rules go, so easy to teach, and can be challenging to any group, but our main reason for wanting it in our program is that it is so much fun, and isn't "good fun" one of the chief objectives of all our recreational and physical education programs? Try it! You'll find your players having lots of fun, and you as an instructor or official getting an equal amount of enjoyment from it.

FIELD DRILLS
FOR THE PRACTICE OF SPEED-A-WAY TECHNIQUES

By Loretta M. Stallings

Although Speed-a-way requires a minimum of technique practice as compared with other team games, there are a number of drills and practice formations which have proved helpful in teaching the game techniques. Some of these are diagrammed here for your use.

Many of the individual techniques of Speed-a-way are similar to those of speedball, i. e., drop kick, lift-up to teammate and self, etc. Excellent drills for the practice of these individual techniques may be found in other sources. [1] However, Speed-a-way is unique in that it allows a player to run with the ball. In order that this technique may be used effectively with the individual techniques mentioned, it requires that drills combining all of these elements be used.

The drills set down here are moving drills rather than stationary, since Speed-a-way is for the most part a running and passing game. They might be called field drills in that they combine those elements which are required for efficient mastery of game techniques on the playing field.

I. SHUTTLE FORMATIONS.

In order that the most benefit may be obtained from the following drills, it is necessary that the smallest possible groups be used. For example, if the squad system is used, each squad or team may be divided into two sections, named A and B. Each of these sections then splits again, one half standing on the 25 yard line; the other half, on the 50 yard line. In this manner a single field may accommodate a comparatively large class, with each girl receiving the maximum of activity.

---

[1] Margaret H. Meyer and Marguerite M. Schwartz, <u>Technic of Team Sports For Women</u>, W. B. Saunders Co., Philadelphia, 1942.

A. DRIBBLE AND PASS, LIFT-UP TO SELF, RUN AND
PASS.

X_1 dribbles the ball forward
and passes to X_2; X_2 lifts
the ball to herself (using any
of the methods, although any
one may be emphasized at a
particular time), runs forward and executes a forward
pass to X_3; X_3 drops the ball
to the ground and dribbles
and passes to X_4. Player
goes to the end of the opposite line.

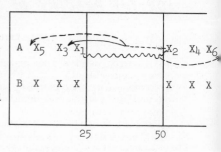

B. DRIBBLE AND PASS, LIFT-UP TO TEAMMATE, RUN
AND PASS.

X_1 dribbles ball forward and
lifts ball to X_2; X_2 catches
ball, runs forward and executes forward pass to X_3;
X_3 drops ball to ground;
dribbles and lifts ball to X_4.
Player goes to end of the
opposite line.

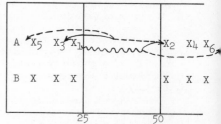

C. PLACE KICK (DROP KICK, PUNT), CATCH, RUN AND
PASS.

X_1 executes place kick from
25 yard line (may be used
also for punt or drop-kick);
X_2 catches ball on fly or after first bounce, runs and
makes forward pass to X_3.
X_1 follows ball forward after
kick. Player goes to end of
opposite line. Note: If
player fails to catch the ball,
she should lift the ball to
herself or to X_3. She should
not pick the ball up and continue play.

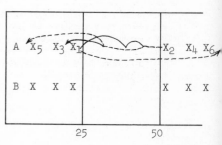

II. FORWARD LINE TECHNIQUES

In order that players may learn to use effective forward line
techniques in playing the ball down the field, and in scoring points,
it is advisable that practice in these combined tactics be had before and during the time players are learning the game. Class

should be divided into equal groups, with five players lined up at
the center line to form the forward line. This line moves together
down the field in executing these techniques. In order that the
minimum of time be spend in waiting, it is best that several balls
be available, so that before one line has completed its run, another line may be started.

A. DRIBBLE, LIFT-UP TO TEAMMATE, RUN AND PASS.

X_1 starts ball with other
forward line players ad-
vancing with her. X_1 attempts lift-up to X_2, who
catches ball and passes down
field to other forward line
players. X_5 moves across
goal line in order to receive
pass for a touchdown. When
X_1 fails to execute a successful lift-up, X_2 receives pass
with her foot, and attempts
to lift-up to X_3, etc. If no
successful lift-up is made,
then last player attempts
field goal.
Note: Short passes ahead of
receiving player should be
emphasized.

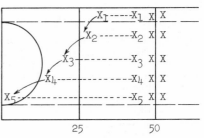

B. STATIONARY DROP KICK FOR POINTS.

Players line-up in semi-
circle facing goal at about
25 yard line. Practice stationary drop-kick. Players
go to end of line on their   X
left. Note: Class mem-   X
bers not participating may
retrieve balls; otherwise,
change retrievers often.
Each line has a ball.

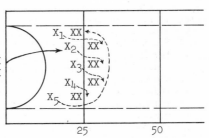

C. RUNNING DROP KICK FOR POINTS.

Since a running drop-kick is more difficult to perform than a
stationary one, and since it is the most effective in a game
situation, it is important that practice in this technique be
had. In executing a running drop-kick, the ball must be drop-
ped further in front of the player than in a stationary kick. It
is a common fault for beginners to drop the ball too close and
thus hit the ball with their knee in attempting the running drop-
kick.

Players line-up at the 25
yard line. Each line is sup-
plied with a ball. Players
run forward a short distance X
and execute a drop-kick for X
points. (Over cross bar between goal posts.) Player
goes to end of line on her
left. Rotate retrievers often.

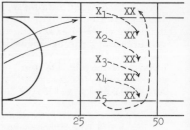

D. DRIBBLE, LIFT-UP TO TEAMMATE, PASS, AND DROP
KICK FOR POINTS.

X_5 dribbles ball forward,
lifts ball to X_4 who passes
ball to X_3; X_3 attempts drop
kick over cross bar and between goal posts. X_2 covers
near goal in case of an unsuccessful kick; catches ball
and passes to X_1 over goal
line for touchdown.
Note: After each round,
start the ball on opposite
end so that each girl may
learn the technique.

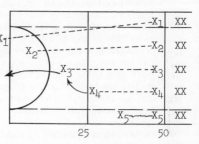

III. DEFENSIVE DRILLS

Although most of the drills mentioned and diagrammed here
are for offensive skills, many such as the punt, drop-kick, and
passes are valuable techniques for defensive fullbacks and halfbacks. Special drills for these players have not been mentioned,
since they may profit by participating in these that have been set
down. After these drills have been practiced, especially those
involving forward line play, it is valuable to have them practiced
against a defensive backfield. In this manner, the forward line
players learn to use their skills against competition, and the backfield players have the opportunity to practice their skills. The
use of the punt and drop-kick by defensive fullbacks cannot be
over-emphasized. It is also important that they learn to lift the
ball to their halfbacks.

It is the conviction of the author that too much time spent in
the practice of individual techniques is not wise. As soon as the
rudiments of such individual techniques as the lift-up, drop-kick,
punt, and forward pass have been learned, then such combined
drills as have been mentioned should be used. In this way, players
may learn to use the skills in conditions that are almost identical
to a game situation, requiring thought as well as skill in executing
techniques. For this reason, these drills have been referred to as
field drills.

SPEED-A-WAY TACTICS

By Kathryn Maloy

Speed-a-way is a game in which the players can do many things with the ball. Running, kicking, and throwing are all basic parts of the game, and how they are combined is generally left to the individual player or teacher.

I have taught Speed-a-way for many years, and perhaps some of the ideas I have used may be of value and may prove helpful in making the game more interesting for the players.

Probably the most disconcerting part, at least to the teacher new to the game, is the way the ball acts as a magnet in attracting all twenty-two players. Every player feels that if she is there, she can certainly help a great deal more by being where the ball is, rather than by playing a position where she is isolated (at least in her own mind) from the play.

As the teacher and the players gain experience in teaching and in playing, the necessity for playing an assigned position becomes apparent; then position play on the field can be emphasized.

Following are briefly the necessary qualifications for each of the positions:

OFFENSIVE PLAYERS

CENTER FORWARD

She is the pivot of the forward line. Play starts with her, and she should be a player who organizes her forward line for a quick thrust at the opponent's goal before the defense can get set. She always stays in the center of the field so that she can aid in passing or in running to either side. She should be a good playmaker and leader; it is not the place for a slow timid player.

INNERS

Inners should have the ability to pass well and to run quickly; it is they who feed the wings and help keep the defensive team spread out so that there are openings for runs or long passes over the goal line to the wings.

Inners should be able to punt when necessary and should be aggressive and alert, especially when near the striking circle. They have excellent chances to intercept fumbled balls and by accurate kicking to score field goals from the circle. They should also be able to drop-kick well.

WINGS

Wings who play their positions on the field, particularly in the alleys, often feel that they are left out of the play. They are the players who usually have the best opportunity of receiving kicks from the fullbacks and thereby start the play up the field much faster. The wings should be fast runners and be particularly good at catching and holding on to the ball. They receive most of the touchdown passes.

DEFENSIVE PLAYERS

THE HALFBACKS

The halfbacks should be fast runners, good kickers, and accurate ball handlers. They should be able to handle the ball well on long hard punts from the opposing backs. It is their duty to guard their opposing forwards as they go beyond the goal line and to knock down touchdown passes in order to prevent scores.

The halfbacks feed the ball to their forwards on free-kicks and follow the ball up to the opposing striking circle, ready to tackle back, and if possible, to intercept defensive passes. The halfbacks are in excellent positions to drop-kick goals and to make long passes for touchdowns.

THE FULLBACKS

The fullbacks' job is almost entirely defensive. They should be aggressive but need not be fast runners. They should be able to punt well and should be able to direct their punts to their inners on or near the center line. The distance and accuracy of their punts often give the wings and inners an advantage on offense by putting them far ahead of their opposing halfbacks.

The fullbacks should not get in the way of the goalie by crowding in front of the goal. The fullbacks are also responsible for guarding the area in the back of the goal; they should be alert to knock down rather than to catch passes behind the goal line.

The fullbacks should not go beyond their opponent's 25 yard line on offensive play, because it leaves too much area for the goalie to cover in case of an intercepted pass or a quick run back by the opponent.

On defense kicks the fullback should lift the ball to a teammate, a halfback, or kick the ball far up the field.

THE GOALIE

The goalie is the Speed-a-way player with the most privileges. She should remember that she may pick up the ball at any time with her hands. She need not wait for the ball to come into the circle or

near the goal area. (A word of caution to the teacher and to the goalie
--do not jeopardize your face or body by trying to pick up a ball when
it is in the center of a group of players.)

The goalie is primarily responsible for the area in front of the
goal; however, her privileges are not confined to the circle. She
should be adept in blocking the ball and clearing out to her fullbacks
or with punts to the forwards.

OFFENSIVE STRATEGY

Goals cannot be scored by a single person against eleven opposing
players; teamwork, therefore, is the keynote to a winning team.

It is fun to be where the ball is, and it is a great temptation to the
wings and the halfbacks (left and right) to gravitate toward the center
of the field, but if the offensive team is to score, it is necessary for
players to remain well-scattered in order to spread out the defense.

One important fact for the forward line to remember is not to go
beyond their own 25 yard line; however, it is better that they do not
go behind the center line. In this way they are ahead of the opposing
halfbacks and are in an advantageous position for receiving defense
kicks from their own backs and goalie.

If the forwards are to play to the team's best advantage, it is better if they do not interfere with the defensive play of their halfbacks,
although, of course, this does not mean that they should not try to intercept passes; their main concern should be to advance the ball up the
field before the opposing defense can get in position to stop them.

Variety in scoring is essential, and it doesn't take the defense
long to discover that a team uses only one way to score. Teachers
should emphasize this fact and have their players practice various
ways to score. If a team has possession of the ball deep into the opponent's territory, at least two forwards should go across the goal
line in order that a forward pass might be made.

The line-up for the kick-off may be varied, but one of the most suc-
successful is below:

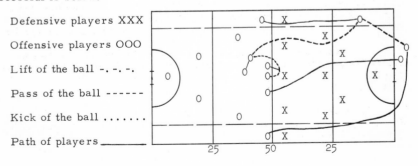

Defensive players XXX

Offensive players OOO

Lift of the ball -.-.-.

Pass of the ball ------

Kick of the ball ....

Path of players _____

25   50   25

The center forward lifts the ball to the left inner who as soon as the whistle is blown, takes a long step or jump forward. The inner then passes to the center half who punts the ball to the left wing. The wing should move down the field rapidly to get behind her right halfback. She can then run with the ball or pass to the right inner who has moved up to be free for a pass or to the right wing, who has run across the goal line and has come across behind the goal. A series of quick passes between the center forward and inners can be used to give the wings time enough to get down the field to receive the kick.

The one thing that cannot be emphasized too much is the necessity of remaining in the right position on the field. It will be necessary to remind the players many times about remaining on their own side of the field.

Quite often the left inner, left wing and the left halfback can score by using quick passes and by running with the ball. The same can be worked with the right side. This type of play can be worked as a general rule when there is a long defense kick to a wing or inner, and if the halfback is an exceptionally fast runner.

A scoring play from out-of-bounds that can be used.

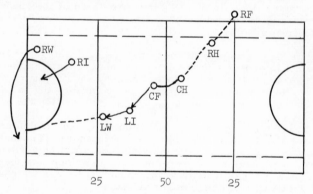

The ball is taken by the right fullback between the twenty-five and fifty yard line. A series of quick passes from one to another may provide scoring opportunity. Offensive players should evade opponents and reach their position at the last possible moment. The right inner and wing should try to position themselves for a field goal or touchdown.

In another play from the center of the field, the forwards stay well ahead of the ball in a V-formation in order to give a better passing attack.

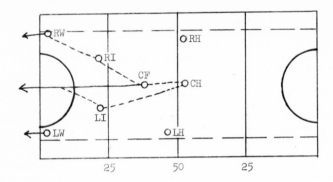

The center half has the ball; with the forwards well ahead of the ball as indicated in the above diagram, she has a number of targets to which she may throw. By skillful maneuvering, the rest of the forward line can be in a position to score a touchdown or a field goal.

A penalty corner can result almost always in a sure goal if the wing lifts the ball to her inner and then receives a pass back immediately before the defensive player can intercept the ball.

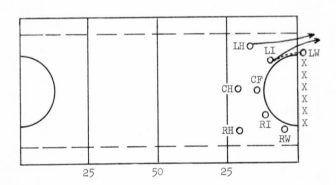

The left wing lifts the ball to her left inner who immediately passes the ball to the left wing or to the left halfback who has crossed the end line.

DEFENSIVE STRATEGY

On the kick-off, the defensive forward should rush the opposing forward line to try to intercept the ball. The forwards should not drop back too far in their attempts to get the ball but should leave most of the guarding to the backs.

The halfbacks should guard the area between the inners and wings closely. The fullbacks should watch for wings going far down the field and should try to intercept kicks or passes to them. They should be in position to receive the ball from their goal keeper and should be able to punt far down the field. The fullbacks are also responsible for the touchdown areas on either side of the goal. Knocking the ball down is much faster than trying to catch it.

On penalty corners a score can be prevented if each of the defending players carefully mark the player that is supposed to be guarded. They should concentrate on the side nearest the ball and watch for quick passes over the goal line. Intercepting rather than preventing passes is the keynote of good defensive players.

Punting or kicking the ball far down the field are the best defensive techniques.

I sincerely hope these suggestions will be helpful to you as a teacher, and that your players get as much enjoyment from playing as have our players.

The players are not perfect; the ball has magnetic tendencies to draw every player to it, but little by little skill comes, and the game becomes a fast, skillful and interesting contest for both players and spectators.

SAFETY IN SPEED-A-WAY

Since Speed-a-way is a game involving much vigorous activity, the safety with which the game is played depends largely upon the instruction of the players and the officiating of the game.

A player should be taught from the start that good position play is an essential safety factor in Speed-a-way. When players play positions rather than the ball, they can control injuries to a greater extent. Little is accomplished by a player who forces her way through a group of players in order to kick the ball except kicked shins or hard body blows from a hard-kicked ball. Good body control and skill in handling the body and fundamentals of running, starting, and stopping quickly should be stressed to eliminate body contact. Players should be taught how to control the ball; to evade and dodge an opponent; to throw the ball; and to lift the ball to another teammate. The technique of guarding or tackling an opponent who is in possession of the ball is most important in the prevention of unnecessary body contact. Team play and its value in preventing injury must be emphasized; players should be safety conscious and at all times should follow safety rules.

During the progress of the game, the referee should be alert to the dangerous elements of the game. All harmful body contact fouls such as obstruction, pushing, charging, tripping, and dangerous kicking (kicking an opponent and kicking the ball directly into an opponent) should be called immediately. The umpire should have control of the game at all times.

It isn't that Speed-a-way is so dangerous; it is the way that it is taught or conducted that can make it dangerous. But if the players are taught body control, team play, deception, and safety rules, and if the umpire has control of the game at all times and does not tolerate harmful fouls, Speed-a-way will be a safe and most enjoyable game.

ILLUSTRATIONS OF FOULS

By Susie Mah

FOULS

Picking up a ground ball
Exception: Goalkeeper

Kicking the opponent

Two players guarding player
in possession of ball

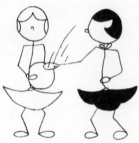

Knocking the ball
from the opponent's
hand.

Pushing

Shoving

Tripping

Dangerously kicking
ball into opponent

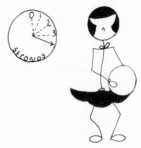

Holding the ball longer than
3 seconds while standing still

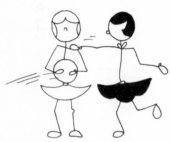

Tagging a player who
receives ball and doesn't move

Standing closer than 5 yds. of
a player taking a throw-in

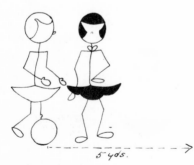

Standing closer than 5 yds. of
a player taking a free-kick

Standing closer than 5 yds. of a
player taking a penalty corner

SPEED-A-WAY TEACHING HINTS

The teaching hints are presented with an idea of making your teaching of Speed-a-way easier. It is realized that some things will work differently for some teachers and for some class, but it is hoped that these hints will be of value to you.

It is suggested that as you use the teaching hints that you keep the following things in mind:

1. That you are interested in acquainting players with the game the first day; consequently, the players will not be experts but they will have fun.

2. That you do not worry about position play or guarding until players are familiar with the game.

3. That you give the fouls and penalties as they occur.

4. That you emphasize the lift-up (kick-up) in order that the ball may be played as an aerial ball.

5. That you emphasize the "do's" and not the "don'ts".

BASIC POINTS TO BE INCLUDED IN THE FIRST DAY OF TEACHING SPEED-A-WAY.

1. Tell your class that it takes two teams of 11 players each to play Speed-a-way; that Speed-a-way is a combination of several games --basketball, field ball, speedball, soccer, hockey, and touch football--consequently, there will be a similarity, yet a difference.

2. OBJECT OF THE GAME

   To advance the ball down the opponent's half of the field in order to score a touchdown or a field goal. The ball may be kicked, passed, or carried (Players may run with the ball as in football.) Demonstrate.

   Note: Emphasize the importance of getting the ball into "your hands", for then you may do anything you want with the ball--run, juggle, pass, drop the ball, kick it, etc. Do not emphasize "kicking" the ball on the ground. (Demonstrate each technique.)

3. SHOW THE WAYS TO CREATE AN AERIAL BALL.

   a. Put foot out and let the ball hit it: Catch the ball directly from the foot or from a bounce.
   Note: The foot does not have to be lifted from the ground.

b. As the ball hits both feet, roll back on heels and pick the ball up from the toes.
   Note: If the ball touches the foot or feet, the ball can be caught while in the air or after one bounce.

c. Squeeze ball between feet, turning feet to the outside and lift.

d. One foot roll and lift the ball up to self.

e. Double foot jump up.

f. Roll ball with one foot to other foot; reach down and pick the ball up (ball is on the foot, not on the ground).

g. One foot lift-up to the teammate (stress this as it is faster and more accurate).

4. SHOW OTHER WAYS TO GET THE BALL (an aerial ball)

a. Getting the ball on the fly from a punt or a throw.

b. Getting the ball after one bounce following a kick (or a touch with the foot).
   Note: Catching a thrown ball on the bounce is not permitted except in junior high school or elementary; catching a kicked ball after one bounce is allowed. Emphasize this. Players will have difficulty with this rule at first.
   Note: If the ball is on the ground, do not pick it up. Only the goal keeper may do this.

5. HOW TO SCORE

Two methods (demonstrate each).

a. Touchdown--2 points

   Players may run over the goal line with the ball or may pass the ball over the end line to a teammate.
   Note: If play occurs between the goal posts, no score.

b. Field Goal--3 points

   Kicking the ball from within the striking circle into the goal cage or between the goal posts.

6. RUNNING WITH THE BALL

If a player has the ball in her hands, and if she is not surrounded, tell her to run. Then tell the other players that if a player has the ball, guard her; if she is running, tag her.

Note: When introducing Speed-a-way, give the penalties as they occur. Thus you do not tell what the penalty is for being tagged until the situation occurs. Remember, you are giving the basic rules so players can play the first day.

7. LINE-UP AND KICK-OFF POSITIONS

   a. Have players line-up in closed formation.

   b. Rather than worrying about names the first day, you might let the players be known as one of the fives (forward line), one of the three's (half), or two's (fullbacks) and goalkeeper.

   c. Tell how the game is started--with a kick-off, all players five yards away from the kicker--all players in their own half of the field.

8. OTHER TEACHING HINTS AFTER YOU HAVE GIVEN THE BASIC IDEA OF THE GAME.

   a. Do not worry about position play or guarding until players have become familiar with the game.

      1. If there are too many players in one spot, stop the play and tell the players to spread out.

      2. You might say, all red fives in this ----> direction; all yellow fives in this <---- direction; red three's this way; yellow three's this other way, etc.

      3. Players will tend to crowd, but they will soon learn the disadvantage of this.

   b. Keep stressing the "lift-up" (particularly the lift-up to a teammate) and (roll up on foot), since it is important that players get the ball into their hands.
   Note: Do not emphasize kicking or dribbling (other than punting) as Speed-a-way is primarily a passing and running game.

   c. If a player has the ball in her hands, and if she is not surrounded say, "run". Players will tend either to freeze with the ball or they will go to the other extreme and run each time the ball is in their possession.
   Note: If a player moves and then she stands still, she can be tagged.

d. Fouls and Penalties

1. In giving the basic rules of the game, you have told the class that they should get the ball into their hands; how to get the ball into their hands, how to score, when to run with the ball, how to tag a running player and how to start the game. As a foul occurs, such as tagging a running player or picking up a ground ball, explain the foul and give the penalty. The majority of penalties will be a free kick on the spot.

2. In the explanation of how to take the free kick, you might say, "one of the red three's gets a free kick". "Red fives ahead." Explain how the free kick is to be taken; all players five yards away, and how the ball should be lifted to a teammate rather than a hard kick forward.

e. Drills versus no drills

You will note that there have been no organized drills given in the introduction of Speed-a-way. If players have a basic understanding of the game, they will often practice on their own the skills which are necessary. This is one of the reasons for letting players play the first day.

Thus these teaching hints show how Speed-a-way can be played on the first day.

SPEED-A-WAY TEACHING HINTS

SECOND DAY

1. REVIEW INFORMATION GIVEN THE PREVIOUS DAY.

a. The ways to create an aerial ball.

Particularly the following:

1. One foot lift-up to the teammate.
2. Roll-up on own foot (or feet, getting the ball directly from the toes).
3. Catching a kicked ball from the fly or one bounce.
   Note: Again emphasize that if the ball is thrown, it must be caught on the fly. Exception: goalkeeper or elementary or junior high students.

b. The need for practice on "lift-ups".

c. Review of a "ground ball" and the penalty for picking up a ground ball.

    d.   Review of "running" with the ball, the ways of stopping a running player, and the penalty for being tagged.

    e.   "Scoring" and the ways to score touchdowns and field goals.

2.   INFORMATION AND DEMONSTRATIONS OF THE TYPES OF KICKS.

    a.   Punt

    b.   Drop-kick

    c.   Place-kick

    Note: Point out which players should be good punters.

3.   POSITION PLAY OF THE FIVE'S, THREE'S, TWO'S, AND GOALKEEPER.

    Note: Names such as wings, inners, center, halfbacks, fullbacks have not yet been given.

    a.   Five's (forward line) play from 50 yard line to opponent's goal line.

    b.   Three's (halfbacks) play from own goal line to opponent's 25 yard line (sometimes to goal line to score).

    c.   Two's (fullbacks) play from own goal line to 50 yard line.
         Note: The game moves so quickly that fullbacks seldom go further than the fifty yard line.

    d.   Goalkeeper may play any place on the field, but it is best that she remain nearer her own goal.

    e.   Emphasize the importance of keeping players spread out.

        1.   Better opportunities to run for touchdowns.

        2.   Easier to pass.

        3.   Easier to create aerial balls.

        4.   Easier to work out scoring plays.
          Note: There are no off-sides in Speed-a-way.

4.   OUT-OF-BOUNDS (as it occurs).

    a.   Side-lines

        Ball may be put in play with a throw-in. All players out of the alley.

    b.   Over the end line.

        Ball is always taken where the circle crosses the end line. May be put in play with a punt, drop-kick, place-kick or throw-in.

Note: If the attacking team puts the ball in play with a throw-in, there must be three passes before a score can be made.

5. BASIC RULES AND PLAYING HINTS.

    a. No rough play or dangerous kicking.
    b. Try to lift the ball into your hands or into your teammate's hands.
    c. If you are clear, run; if not, stand still and pass the ball.
    d. To get the ball out of your territory, punt the ball down the field.
    e. Spread out; do not crowd.
    f. Catch a hard kicked ball on the bounce as it is easier to control.
        Note: Extra players can practice lift-ups and kicks while teams are playing.

6. Remember--you are still acquainting players with the game. Do not worry about marking or good position play yet.

SPEED-A-WAY TEACHING HINTS
THIRD DAY

1. REVIEW INFORMATION GIVEN THE PREVIOUS DAYS.

    a. Ways to create aerial balls.
    b. Types of kicks.
        When the punt, drop-kick and place-kick is used.
    c. Position play of players (not given the correct names).
    d. Review of out-of-bounds.
        What player puts the ball in play.

2. FOULS AND PENALTIES

Explain the fouls and penalties

    a. Outside of the circles.
    b. Inside the circles.
        1. By the defending team.
        2. By the attacking team.
    c. Who puts the ball in play.
    d. Where players stand when a penalty is being taken.

3. OFFENSIVE STRATEGY.

    a. Emphasize position play on the field.
    b. Forward line players waiting ahead in order to set-up a passing attack.
    c. Keeping one or more players over the goal line waiting to receive a pass when the team is trying to score.

    d.   Running with the ball only when there is an opening.
    e.   Use of plays on the kick-off to set-up scoring opportunities.
    f.   Use of the "lift-up" to create aerial balls.

4.   DEFENSIVE STRATEGY.

    a.   Position play and marking.
    b.   Use of interception.
    c.   Use of punt to get the ball away from the goal.
    d.   Use of goalkeeper's special privileges.
    e.   Getting the ball away from the center of the field.

5.   HELPFUL HINTS.

By the third day, the majority of students should have an understanding of the game, the ways to create aerial balls, the main fouls and penalties. Players now need to work on techniques and tactics which will result only from game practice and "teacher correction." Your students will have fun; they will work out plays to score; they will think of ways to keep their opponents from scoring.

Let your students play; give them helpful hints as the situation arises. They will have fun playing Speed-a-way, if you let them play.

ILLUSTRATIONS OF WAYS TO CREATE AERIAL BALLS

By Lois Fiscus and Joyce Malone

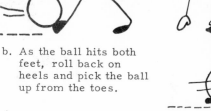

b. As the ball hits both feet, roll back on heels and pick the ball up from the toes.

a. Put foot out and let ball hit it. Catch the ball directly from the foot or from a bounce. The foot does not have to be lifted from the ground.

c. Squeeze the ball between the feet, turning the feet to the outside. The ball must be lifted off the ground.

d. One foot roll and lift up to self.

e. By a two-legged lift-up to one's self. Secure the ball between the ankles, then jump into the air and place the ball in position for catching with the hands before it touches the ground.

26

ILLUSTRATIONS OF WAYS TO CREATE AERIAL BALLS

f. One foot lift-up to a teammate. The ball may be
   caught on the fly or after
   one bounce.

g. Getting the ball after one bounce
   following a kick (or touch with
   the foot).

h. Getting the ball on the fly from a pass.

SPEED-A-WAY

LINE-UP

Girls' Physical Education Department
Edison High School, Stockton, California

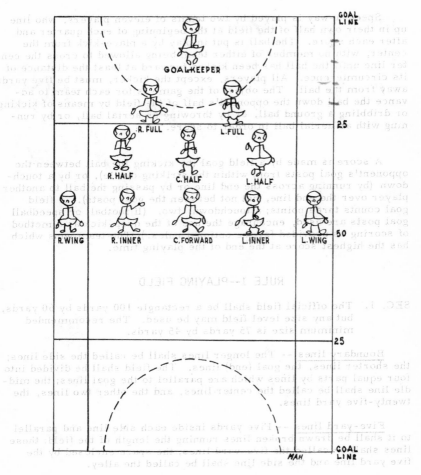

SPEED-A-WAY
(Revised, 1960)

Originated by
Marjorie S. Larsen, Chairman
Girls' Physical Education Department
Edison High School, Stockton, California

Speed-a-way is played by two teams of eleven players, who line up in their own half of the field at the beginning of each quarter and after each score. The ball is put in play by a place-kick from the center, with no member of either team being allowed to cross the center line until the ball has been kicked forward at least the distance of its circumference. All players, except the kicker, must be five yards away from the ball. The object of the game is for each team to advance the ball down the opponent's half of the field by means of kicking or dribbling a ground ball, or by throwing an aerial ball, or by running with an aerial ball in order to score.

A score is made by a field goal (by kicking the ball between the opponent's goal posts from within the striking circle), or by a touchdown (by running across the end line or by passing the ball to another player over the end line, but not between the goal posts). A field goal counts three points; a touchdown, two. (If football or speedball goal posts are used, encourage the use of the drop-kick as a method of scoring as provided for the optional rules.) The team wins which has the highest score at the end of the playing time.

RULE 1--PLAYING FIELD

SEC. 1. The official field shall be a rectangle 100 yards by 60 yards, but any size level field may be used. The recommended minimum size is 75 yards by 45 yards.

Boundary lines -- The longer lines shall be called the side lines; the shorter lines, the goal (end) lines. The field shall be divided into four equal parts by lines which are parallel to the goal lines; the middle line shall be called the center lines, and the other two lines, the twenty-five yard lines.

Five-yard lines -- Five yards inside each side line and parallel to it shall be drawn broken lines running the length of the field; these lines shall be called the five-yard lines; the space enclosed by the five yard line and the side line shall be called the alley.

Striking circles -- In front of each goal parallel to the goal line and fifteen yards from it, shall be drawn a line four yards in length. From each end of this line shall be drawn a quarter circle to a point on the end line, fifteen yards from each goal post, using the goal post as a center of each quarter circle. The space enclosed by these lines, including the lines themselves, shall be called the striking circle.

- 28 -

Note: Where fields are reduced in size, the 25 yard lines shall be 25 yards from the goal lines; the five-yard lines, five yards from the side lines, and the circles, the regulation size.

SEC. 2. THE GOALS

The goal shall be the center of each goal line and shall consist of two posts four yards apart (inside measurements), joined together by a horizontal crossbar seven feet from the ground. Four feet back of the goal, other posts and a crossbar shall be erected and joined to the goal; wire shall be used to enclose the space.

Note 1: Speed-a-way can be adapted to any playing field that is available. If the field is equipped with soccer or speedball goal posts, or football goal posts, or field hockey cages, then these may be used in substitution for the goal posts recommended for Speed-a-way. It is possible to use benches, towels, or any safe materials in order to make a goal area.

Note 2: Speed-a-way goal posts have the same measurements as those in field hockey.

RULE 2--PLAYERS AND EQUIPMENT

SEC. 1. THE TEAMS

A. The Players:

Speed-a-way is played by two teams of eleven players, designated as five forwards (forward line), namely: left wing, left inner, center forward, right inner, and right wing; the backfield--three half-backs, namely: left, center, and right; two fullbacks, namely: left and right; and one goalkeeper.

Note: A team may play with less than eleven players, but it is not recommended.

B. The Captains:

1. Shall furnish the scorekeeper with the names and positions of their players before the game.
2. Shall have the option of putting the ball in play or of selecting their goal when winning the toss of a coin.
3. Shall have the choice of kicking off or of receiving after a goal has been scored against them.

Note: If a team elects to receive, this does not mean that the opponents must kick the ball to them.

4. Shall confer with the umpire regarding the length of playing time, which may be shortened by mutual consent.

5. Shall appoint a substitute captain to act during the time the regular captain is not playing.
6. Shall be the representative of her team in the questioning of any decisions, etc.

C. Substitutes:

Substitutes may be put into the game for players who for any reason have been taken out. A substitute may be put into the game only when the ball is not in play. Time-our may not be called for substitution. A player who has been taken out of the game for any reason other than disqualification may be allowed to re-enter the game twice. A substitute shall report to the scorekeeper, and then be recognized by the nearest Umpire, who shall send her in at the first dead ball.

Penalty: In case a player fails to report to the proper officials or in case a player re-enters the game more than twice (that player shall also be disqualified from the game), the opposing team shall be given possession of the ball in the manner that play oridinarily would have resumed, i. e., a throw-in, a free-kick, etc. If a penalty corner has been awarded, and it is the attacking team who violates the substitute rule, then the defending team shall be awarded a free kick anywhere in the striking circle; or if the defending team has been awarded a free kick in the striking circle, play shall be resumed with a penalty corner for the attacking team. However, if play was from the end line because of the out-of-bounds rule, then the opposing team would put the ball in play from the end line.

SEC. 2. EQUIPMENT

A. The official ball shall be a regulation speed-a-way ball.

Note: A soccer ball can be used, but the speed-a-way ball is of a different size and texture; it bounces higher and is more easily controlled and handled.

B. Light shin guards may be worn for leg protection.
C. Each team should wear a distinguishing color. The goalkeeper should be distinguished from other members of her team, since she has additional playing privileges. If pinnies are worn, the goalkeeper could tie hers around the waist or arm or some place where it can be easily seen to make her identification easy.

RULE 3--OFFICIALS

SEC. 1. The officials for an official game shall be two Umpires, four Linesmen, a Time-keeper, and a Scorekeeper.

SEC. 2. Each Umpire shall take one-half of the field without changing ends. Each Umpire shall take the entire side line on one side of the field for the throw-in and call fouls in the same territory when in her opinion they have not been visible to the other Umpire.

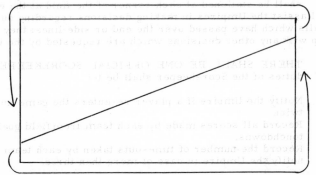

The official should be responsible for the area to her right and the corner to her left.

SEC. 3. Before the beginning of the game, the Umpires shall decide which one will instruct the Scorekeeper and the Captains (or the teams) before the game, and which Umpire shall put the ball in play at the beginning of each quarter and after a goal has been scored.

SEC. 4. THE UMPIRE SHALL:

    a. Make all decisions for infringement of rules committed outside or inside the boundary lines.

Note: Enforcing Rules: An Umpire shall refrain from putting the provision of any rule into effect in cases where she is satisfied that by enforcing it she would be giving an advantage to the team which fouled.

    b. See that all kick-offs, free-kicks, penalty corners, and throw-ins are properly taken.

Note: Umpires should indicate by use of an arm signal which team is to put the ball in play. Point the arm in the direction that the team is going.

    c. Use her whistle at the beginning of the game and before each succeeding kick-off, including that at the beginning of each quarter.

d. Use her whistle to signify that the ball is out of play.
e. Use her whistle to put the ball into play only in the case of
    a kick-off.
f. Use her whistle to signify a field goal or a touchdown has
    been scored.
g. Indicate to the Scorekeeper the player who scored.
h. Remove any player for unsportsmanlike conduct or for un-
    necessary roughness.

SEC. 5. FOUR LINESMEN SHALL ASSIST IN ALL GAMES. They
shall be stationed at each corner of the field at the end lines
and shall assist the Umpires in making decisions regarding out-of-
bound balls which have passed over the end or side lines; they shall
also help with any other decisions which are requested by the Umpires.

SEC. 6. THERE SHALL BE ONE OFFICIAL SCOREKEEPER. The
duties of the Scorekeeper shall be to:

a. Notify the Umpire if a player re-enters the game more than
    twice.
b. Record all scores made by each team from field goals or
    touchdowns.
c. Record the number of time-outs taken by each team and
    notify the Umpire in case of more than three.

Penalty: In case there is an infringement of this rule, the opposing team shall be given possession of the ball in the manner that play
oridinarily would have been resumed, i. e., a throw-in, a free-kick.
If a penalty corner is to take place, and it is the attacking team who
violates the substitute rule, the defending team shall be awarded a
free kick at the edge of the striking circle; or if the defending team
has been awarded a free kick at the edge of the striking circle, play
shall be resumed with a penalty corner for the attacking team. If the
play was from the end-line because of the out-of-bounds rule (not the
penalty corner rule), then the opposing team would put the ball in
play from the end line.

SEC. 7. THERE SHALL BE ONE OFFICIAL TIMEKEEPER. The
duties of the Timekeeper shall be to:

a. Keep account of playing time.
b. Subtract time taken for time-out.
c. Signify by means of a whistle the end of each playing period.

Note: The whistle of the Timekeeper indicates the end of each playing
period. If the ball is in the air on the way to a goal or a touchdown when the whistle blows for the end of the playing time, a
score if made does not count.

RULE 4--PLAYING TERMS AND PRIVILEGES

SEC. 1.   GENERAL

A.   Attacking team

The term used to designate the players of the team which has possession of the ball, or which, when the play nears a goal, is attempting to score.

B.   Defending team

The term used to designate the players of the team which does not have possession of the ball, or which, when the ball nears their own goal, is attempting to prevent the opponent from scoring.

C.   Own goal

The goal which a team defends.

D.   Own half of the field

That section of the field from the center line to the goal line in which the team's own goal is situated.

Before each kick-off, the players of each team line-up on the playing field in their respective halves of the field and face their opponent's goal. All players except the kicker must be five yards away from the ball.

Note: Players are not required to be away from the center line but just five yards away from the ball.

E.   Aerial Ball

An aerial ball is one that has been raised into the air by a kick with the foot.

Note 1:   A kicked ball which takes only one bounce may be picked up and played as an aerial ball. If the ball touches the foot in any way, the ball may then be caught on the fly or on one bounce.

Note 2:   A ball which is thrown and which takes one bounce cannot be played as an aerial ball. (Exception: Goalkeeper and for those playing in the junior high school (7th and 8th grades) and the elementary level.)

Note 3:   If a player touches an aerial ball with her hands, and the ball then touches the ground, the ball must be played as a ground ball.

Interpretation: A player attempts to catch a ball that has been kicked; she fumbles the ball; it falls to the ground. The ball must be played as a ground ball.

F.   Ground Ball

A ground ball is one that is rolling, is stationary on the ground, or which is bouncing (has bounced more than once). Such a ball cannot be picked up or touched by the hands of any player except the goalkeeper.

Interpretation: A ground ball may be converted to an aerial ball only by the feet.

Note: A ball kicked into the air remains an aerial ball until it has been fumbled to the ground or has bounced more than once. A thrown ball becomes a ground ball immediately upon contact with the ground. (Exception: Goalkeeper and for those playing in the junior high school (7th and 8th grades) and in the elementary level, a ball which is thrown and which takes only one bounce can be played as an aerial ball.

G.   Kick-off

A kick-off is the means of putting the ball in play with a place kick from the center at the start of each quarter and after each score. The ball must move forward the distance of its circumference. It may be lifted to a teammate and does not have to be kicked in such a way to enable the opponents to gain possession.

H.   Pivot

A pivot is a play in which a player who is holding the ball steps once or more than once in any direction with the same foot, the other foot (called the pivot foot) being kept at its initial point of contact with the ground.

Interpretation: If the pivot foot is lifted, this constitutes moving with the ball, and the player can be tagged.

SEC. 2.   TECHNIQUES

A.   Kicking

1.   Drop-kick

A drop-kick is a play in which a player drops the ball and kicks it immediately after it strikes the ground.

2. Place-kick

  A place-kick is a play in which a player, with or
without preliminary steps, kicks the ball which is stationary on the ground. The ball may be lifted into the
air or kept on the ground.

Note:1: A place-kick is used for a kick-off or a free-kick; it may also
be used when the ball goes out-of-bounds over the end-line or
if there is a penalty corner. All players except the kicker
must be five yards away from the ball.

Note 2: If a free-kick has been awarded, a punt or drop-kick cannot
be used.

3. Punt

  A punt is a play in which a player drops the ball
and kicks it before it strikes the ground. Any player
is privileged to use the punt.

4. Dribble

  A dribble is a succession of kicks forward in which
the player keeps the ball under control with the feet and
advances it.

B. Throwing

  Throwing is a means of advancing the ball in the air by
a one or two-handed pass.

Note: A thrown ball may not be caught after it has touched the ground.
(Exception: goalkeeper and (elementary and junior high players).

C. Juggle

  A juggle is a play in which a player tosses the ball in
the air to herself. A player may move the ball by a series
of juggles with one or both hands.

D. Stopping the ball

1. Blocking the ball

  Blocking the ball is interrupting the progress of a
ground ball with any part of the body, except with the
hands (Exception: Goalkeeper).

Note: A ball which has been kicked (touched by the foot) and which has
taken but one bounce (aerial ball) may be blocked with the hands.

2.   Trapping the ball

Trapping the ball is stopping its flight by securing it under the foot, between both feet, or between the front of the legs and the ground.

Note: Trapping the ball does not necessarily give a player possession of the ball. It may be kicked out from her legs or feet; however, dangerous kicking should be called if personal contact results.

3.   Volley

A volley is a play in which a player meets a ball with some part of the body such as the head, hip, shoulder, knee or foot.

Note: A ground ball may not be converted into an aerial ball by any part of the body except by the foot. If a bouncing ball (ball which has bounced more than once) touches the knee or any other part of the body except the foot, it is not legal to play the ball as an aerial ball.

SEC. 3.   PLAYING PRIVILEGES

a.   The ball may be caught or otherwise played with the hands whenever it is an aerial ball.

Note: A kicked ball (any ball which touches the foot) which is caught on the fly or on the first bounce may be played as an aerial ball. A kicked ball which is rolling or which has bounced more than once cannot be picked up with the hands. (Exception: Goal-keeper.)

Penalty: For any breach of this rule, a free-kick shall be awarded the opponent where the foul occurred. (Exception: if the foul occurs in the striking circle. See Rule 9.)

b.   A ground ball may be converted into an aerial ball only with the feet. (Exception: Goalkeeper.)

The following methods may be used to convert a ground ball into an aerial ball:

1.   By a lift-up (kick-up) to one's self or to another player; i.e., placing the foot under the ball and lifting it into the air from its ground position so that it may be caught (or intercepted) before touching the ground.

2.   By a lift-up (kick-up) to one's self; i.e., snapping one foot from the top of the ball (as is done with a racket in picking up a tennis ball).

3. By a two-legged lift-up (kick-up) to one's self; i.e., by securing the ball between the ankles, then jumping into the air and placing the ball in position for catching with the hands before it touches the ground.

<u>Note:</u> This type of lift-up is generally too slow a method.

4. By allowing an oncoming ball to roll onto one's instep and then with a slight kick, lifting the ball into the air so that it may be caught with the hands.

5. By putting a foot out and letting the ball hit it. Catch the ball directly from the foot or from a bounce.

<u>Note:</u> The foot does not have to be lifted from the ground.

6. By lifting the toes up of both feet as the ball hits both feet and then picking the ball up from the toes.

<u>Note:</u> If the ball touches the foot or feet, the ball can be caught while in the air or after one bounce.

7. Squeeze ball between feet, turning feet to the outside. Ball must be lifted off the ground.

8. Roll ball with one foot to the other foot; reach down and pick the ball up. (Ball is on the foot, not on the ground.)

c. A player may not bounce a ball and catch it.

d. A player who has legally caught a ball may run with the ball, throw the ball to her teammate, punt, or drop-kick the ball, or drop the ball and play it as a ground ball, or she may juggle it.

e. A player who is standing still when catching the ball from a kick or a throw or a juggle may hold the ball for three seconds without penalty or without the liability of being tagged. Once a player has moved with the ball, she may be tagged on the back by an opponent as long as the ball is retained in her hands. However, if a player has moved with the ball, she is not allowed to stop without the liability of being tagged.

<u>Note 1:</u> One or both hands may be used to tag a player on the back. The opposing team is awarded a free-kick whenever a player is legally tagged; however, if a defending player is tagged in the circle, then a penalty corner is awarded.

<u>Note 2:</u> A pivot (in which the pivot foot does not leave the ground) does not constitute a move.

f. A player may legally guard an opponent who has the ball. Guarding with the arms in any plane is permitted as long as no contact with either the opponent's person or with the ball results. A player with the ball may be guarded by only one person.

Note: If the player with the ball is guarded by more than one person, and she is unable to make a successful play, a foul is called. See Rule 9.

Penalty: For an infringement of this rule, a free-kick (or penalty corner) is awarded the team who has possession of the ball.

Note: An umpire shall refrain from putting the provision of any rule into effect in cases where she is satisfied that by enforcing it she would be giving an advantage to the team that committed the infringement.

g. A player may juggle the ball any number of times, moving or standing still, and may be tagged only when she has held the ball three seconds.

Note: A juggle may be intercepted or blocked without personal contact by any opposing player.

SEC. 4. THE GOALKEEPER'S PRIVILEGES

a. The goalkeeper may handle the ball with her hands at any time at any place on the field.

b. She may play a ball at any time with her hands or feet regardless whether it is a ground ball or an aerial ball.

c. Her privileges are not confined to the circle. She may go any place on the field and still retain her privileges.

d. The goalkeeper may score.

Note: The goalkeeper should wear something to distinguish her from other members of her team.

RULE 5--THE GAME

SEC. 1. The game shall consist of four quarters of eight minutes each with a two minute rest interval between the first and second and third and fourth quarters, and a ten-minute interval between halves. The periods may be shortened by mutual consent of the captains and the officials. (Shortened periods are advocated for high schools girls.)

SEC. 2. The winner of the toss shall have the choice of either putting the ball in play or of selecting the goal which the team is to defend. At the beginning of each quarter, thereafter, the kick-off shall be taken by the team which did not kick-off at the beginning of the previous quarter.

SEC. 3.   Goals shall be changed at half-time.

SEC. 4.)   The game shall be commenced by a kick-off from the center of the field in the direction of the opponent's goal.

Note: A kick-off means that the ball may be kicked forward to the opponents or may be lifted to a teammate who does not cross the center line before the ball has been kicked forward.

The ball must be kicked forward at least the distance of its own circumference and may be lifted by the foot to a teammate. The player who kicked the ball may not touch it again until it has first been touched by another player. All players except the kicker must be five yards away from the ball. Players may stand on but not over the center line. No opponent shall cross the center line, nor shall any teammate of the one taking the kick-off cross the center line until the ball has been kicked.

Note: If the player in the center takes the kick-off before the whistle is blown, the play is taken over again by the same player.

Penalty: For an infringement of the rule on the kick-off, a free-kick shall be awarded to the opponent at the spot where the foul occurred. (If the opponent crosses the center line before the ball is kicked but gains no advantage, a foul should not be called.)

Note: Since a free-kick has been awarded, free-kick rules apply. See Rule 10.

SEC. 5.)   Following a score, the team which is scored upon shall have its choice of kicking off or of letting the opponents kick off.

RULE 6--TIME-OUT

SEC. 1.)   Time-out may be taken only by the team which has possession of the ball and when the ball is dead, or any time in case of injury, or at the discretion of the Umpire. Time-out may be called by any player.

SEC. 2.   Time-out may be taken only when ordered by the Umpire.

SEC. 3.   Three time-outs of one minute each shall be allowed each team during a game. A fourth and succeeding time-out shall constitute a team foul. Three team fouls disqualify a team.

Penalty: For an infringement of this rule, the opposing team shall be given possession of the ball in the manner that play ordinarily would have been resumed. See Rule 2, Sec. C.

SEC. 4.   The ball shall be put in play in the following manner following a time-out:

   a.   If the ball is out-of-bounds when time-out is called, it shall be put in play from out-of-bounds to the team entitled to it.

   b.   If time-out is requested just after a goal has been made, the play shall be resumed by a kick-off.

   c.   If time-out is requested just after a foul is called, play shall be resumed by putting into effect the penalty for the foul.

   d.   If the ball is in possession of a player when time is called, that player shall take the ball out-of-bounds at the side line nearest the spot where the ball was when time-out was taken.

RULE 7--SCORING

SEC. 1.   A field goal counts three points; a touchdown, two points.

SEC. 2.   A field goal shall be scored when a ground ball is kicked by a member of the attacking team from within the striking circle, so that the ball passes over the goal line, between the goal posts and under the crossbar. If such a ball is last touched by a defending player, the goal shall count for the attacking side. If the ball is legally touched by the hands of any player, no member of the attacking side can score a field goal until the ball has touched the ground and then has been played as a ground ball. Consequently, a punt through the goal posts does not count.

METHODS OF SCORING

1.   Field goal
        Kicking the ball between the opponent's goal post from within the striking circle.
2.   Touchdown
     a.   Running across the end line with the ball.
     b.   Passing the ball to another player over the end line.

Note: A field goal cannot be scored directly from a penalty corner or from a free-kick.

Note: A drop-kick under the crossbar will count as a field goal if made from within the striking circle (three points).

SEC. 3. A touchdown shall be scored by the completion of a forward pass, the ball being thrown by an attacking player who is any place on the field, and is caught and held by a teammate who is behind the goal line, which extends from side line to side line with the exception of the part between the goal posts. A pass received by a player standing behind the goal line between the goal posts does not score, and the ball is awarded to the defending team out-of-bounds.

Note 1: The receiver must be completely over the goal line for the score to count.

Note 2: If the forward pass is incomplete, out-of-bounds rules apply. See out-of-bounds rules, Rule 12.)

Note 3: If a throw-in has been made from the end line or from the side line between the defending team's 25-yard line and the goal line, there must be three passes before a touchdown may be scored; i. e., Player A who is out-of-bounds throws the ball to teammate B who is in the field. Player B throws the ball to Player C; Player C throws the ball across the goal line to any of her teammates to score.

Penalty: For an infringement of this rule, the opponent shall be awarded a throw-in to be taken where the play originally started, unless the ball from the end line has been played as a penalty corner, in which case the defending team would get a free-kick at the edge of the circle.

Note 4: If a lift-up (kick-up) has been made from the end line by a player to a teammate who is in the field, three passes are not necessary to score a touchdown.

SEC. 4. A touchdown also shall be scored by a player running over the goal line, which extends from the side line to side line, with the exception of the part between the goal posts. A player running over the goal line between the goal posts does not score, and the ball is awarded to the defending team out-of-bounds. Out-of-bound rules apply. See Rule 12.

SEC. 5. Option rule for use of the drop-kick over the crossbar. In case goal posts are the same as those used for soccer, speedball, or football (crossbar is higher than that used in the hockey cage), then a drop-kick, with the ball passing between the goal posts and over the crossbar shall score four points. The drop-kick may be made from any place on the playing field.

Note: If the drop-kick is used and the ball goes under the crossbar, a field goal is scored instead, and only three points are scored.

However, in this case, the ball must have been kicked from within the striking circle; if not, out-of-bounds rules would apply.

SEC. 6.   If a forward pass is legally intercepted by a defensive player who is behind the goal line, the ball shall be awarded to the defending team out-of-bounds. If the ball touches the ground in-bounds in an unsuccessful effort by the attacking team to score a touchdown, the ball shall remain in play until a score is made or until the ball goes out-of-bounds, or until the ball is otherwise declared dead. If the ball is thrown between the goal posts, a goal is not scored and out-of-bound rules apply. (See Rule 12.)

SEC. 7.   If a player is in the act of catching a pass over the end line, and she is deliberately fouled causing her to loss the ball, a touchdown shall automatically be awarded her team.

SEC. 8.   After a score has been made, the ball shall be returned to the center with the team being scored against having its choice of kicking-off or of letting the opponent kick-off.

RULE 8--TIE BALL

SEC. 1.) In case a ball is held by two opposing players simultaneously, the Umpire shall declare a tie ball. The Umpire shall toss-up the ball between the two contesting players who may hit the ball with one or both hands. Neither of the contesting players may play the ball until it has touched the ground or has been played by some other player. If a tie ball occurs at a point less than five yards from the end lines or the side lines, the ball shall be tossed up at a spot five yards from the lines opposite from where the tie occurred.

Note 1: When a player thinks she has tied a ball but in the Umpire's opinion the other player gained possession of it first, the Umpire shall award a free-kick to that player. (If this oc- curs in a circle, then a free-kick at the edge of the circle or penalty corner rule would apply.)

Note 2: If a player has possession of a ball and an opponent places one or both hands on the ball in an attempt to tie the ball, then a free-kick shall be awarded to the team originally in possession of the ball.

Note 3: A player may not score directly from a toss-up.

Interpretation: A player jumping for a tossed ball may not tap the ball directly to a teammate over the goal line in order to score.

Penalty: For an infringement of this rule a free-kick shall be awarded to the opponent at the spot where the play originally started.

Exception: If the foul occurred within the striking circle, see Rule 9.

RULE 9--FOULS

SEC. 1. A foul is an infringement of any rule of the game.

A. Players shall not:

1. Pick up a ground ball (Exception: Goalkeeper).
2. Hold the ball longer than three seconds after receiving the ball. (Exception: A player who is running with the ball.)
3. Tag a player who receives the ball and does not move. A pivot does not constitute a move.
4. Two players or more shall not guard a player who is in possession of the ball.

Note: A foul is called if the player with the ball cannot make a successful play.

5. Trip, shove, push, charge, strike at her opponent, except to tag a player on the back only when the latter is running with the ball.
6. Knock the ball from her opponent's hand.
7. Kick her opponent or dangerously kick the ball into her opponent.
8. Stand closer than five yards to the ball on the kick-off.
9. Stand closer than five yards to the player taking a penalty corner.
10. Stand closer than five yards to a player who is taking a throw-in or a free-kick.
11. Play the ball after taking a throw-in or a free-kick until the ball has been played by another player.
12. Run for a touchdown immediately upon receiving the ball from a throw-in which has occurred from the end line or from within the opponent's 25 yard line and own goal line.

Note: If a throw-in is made from the side line between the defending team's 25 yard line and goal line, or from the goal line, there must be three passes before a touchdown can be scored.

13. Score directly from a free-kick, throw-in, or a toss-up.

Penalty:
Outside the circles.

For any breach, the penalty shall be a free-kick for the opposing team at the spot where the infringement occurred.

Inside the circles.

1. For any breach by the attacking team, the penalty shall be a free-kick for the defending team from any point inside the circle.

2. For any breach by the defending team, the penalty shall be a penalty corner. (See Rule 11.)

Note 1: For rough play or misconduct, the Umpire shall have discretionary power to warn the offending player or to suspend her from the game.

Note 2: In case of a foul, the Umpire shall refrain from putting the provision of any rule into effect in cases where she is satisfied that by enforcing it she would be giving an advantage to the team that committed the foul.

Interpretation: Player A receives the ball from her teammate, and she does not move; Player B in her excitement accidentally tags Player A. It would be giving an advantage to Player B to call a penalty against her, since giving Player A a free-kick is more of a disadvantage than it is for her to maintain possession of the ball in her hands.

SEC. 2. A double foul is an infringement of the rules committed simultaneously by a member of both teams for which a toss-up is awarded. The toss-up is awarded on the spot, unless it occurs nearer than five yards to the end-line or the side lines, in which case it is brought to a spot opposite the place where the foul occurred, five yards from the side or end lines. (A goal cannot be scored directly from a toss-up. (See Rule 8.)

SEC. 3. Anything which is not specifically prohibited by the rules may be done.

RULE 10--FREE-KICK

SEC. 1. A team which is awarded a free-kick for an infringement of a rule shall put the ball in play by a place-kick where the foul occurred. (Exception: When a free-kick is awarded for a foul within the striking circle.)

a. No player shall be within five yards of the ball until the kick is taken.

Note: If an opponent stands closer than five yards on a free-kick and no advantage is gained, play continues.

b. Play begins when the ball is kicked.
c. The ball must travel at least the distance of its circumference. It may be kicked in any direction.
d. The ball may be lifted (kicked-up) to another player.
e. The kicker shall not play the ball again until it is played by another player.

Penalty: For an infringement of the free-kick rule, a free-kick shall be awarded the opponent at the place where the infringement occurred. (Exception: If the foul occurs within the striking circle, see Rule 9.

f. A field goal or a touchdown cannot be scored directly from a free-kick.

RULE 11--PENALTY CORNER

SEC. 1. A penalty corner is awarded the attacking team if the defending team commits a foul in its own circle. A wing of the attacking team shall put the ball in play from a point on the goal line 15 yards from the nearer goal posts (where the circle bisects the end line) with a throw-in, a punt, a place-kick, or a drop-kick. At the moment of play, the rest of the attacking team must be outside the circle in the field of play; the backfield players of the defending team must be behind their own goal line; and the rest of the defending team shall stand on or beyond the nearer 25 yard line. No player shall stand within five yards of the ball when the penalty corner is taken, nor may the player making the play be allowed to touch the ball until it has been touched by another player.

Note 1: If the throw-in is used, there must be three passes before a touchdown may be scored; i.e., Player A, who is out-of-bounds, throws the ball to teammate B, who is in the field. Player B throws the ball to Player C; Player C throws the ball across the goal line to any of her teammates to score.

Penalty: For an infringement of the rule by the defending team, the penalty corner shall be taken again.

Note 2: If any type of kick is used on the penalty corner, then the three pass rule does not apply.

For an infringement of the rule by the attacking team, the Umpire shall give a free-kick to the defending team; this kick may be taken anywhere in the circle.

RULE 12--OUT-OF-BOUNDS

SEC. 1. OVER THE SIDE-LINES.

a. When the ball passes wholly over the side lines, it shall be a throw-in by the opponent of the player who last touched it.
b. The player throwing the ball must stand behind the side line and may throw the ball with any type of one-handed or two-handed pass. The ball shall be in play when it has left the player's hands and may be played as an aerial or a ground ball. The thrower shall not play the ball until it has been played by another player. All players must be out of the alley until the ball has left the thrower's hands. No goal may be scored directly from a throw-in.

LINE-UP FOR A PENALTY CORNER

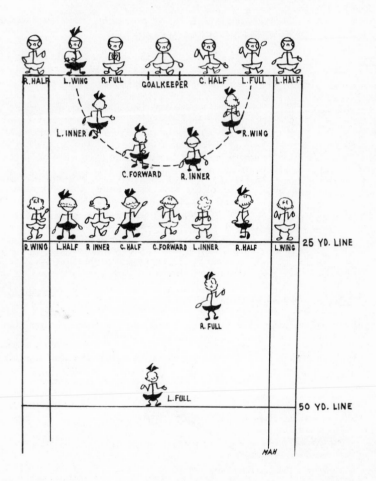

R.HALF L.WING R.FULL GOALKEEPER C.HALF L.FULL L.HALF

L.INNER R.WING

C.FORWARD R.INNER

R.WING L.HALF R INNER C.HALF C.FORWARD L.INNER R.HALF L.WING 25 YD. LINE

R. FULL

L.FULL 50 YD. LINE

MAH

Penalty:

1. For a breach of the rule by the player taking the throw-in or by her teammate, the throw-in shall be taken by a player of the opposite team.

2. For a breach of the rule by an opponent, the throw-in shall be taken again.

Note: If a throw-in has been made from the side line between the defending team's 25-yard line and the goal line, there must be three passes before a touchdown can be scored.

Penalty: For an infringement of the rule by the team who throws the ball in, the opponent shall be awarded a throw-in to be taken where the play originally started.

SEC. 2. OVER THE END-LINE

a. If the ball is sent over the goal line, not between the goal posts, by a player of the attacking team, the ball shall be taken by the defending player at a point 15 yards from the goal posts on the side that the ball went out (where the circle bisects the end-line). The ball may be put in play with a throw-in, a punt, a place-kick or a drop-kick. All players must be five yards away from the ball. The player taking the kick or throw-in, may not play the ball until the ball has been played by another player.

Penalty: For an infringement of the rule by the player making the play, the ball shall be awarded to the opponent at the spot where the play originally started.

b. If the ball is sent over the goal line, not between the goal posts by a player of the defending team, the ball shall be taken by the opponent at a point 15 yards from the goal posts (where the circle bisects the goal line) on the side that the ball went out. The ball may be put in play with a throw-in, a punt, place-kick or a drop-kick. All players must be five yards away.

Note: If a throw-in is used, there must be three passes before a touchdown can be scored.

Penalty: If three passes are not used to score a touchdown in an out-of-bounds play from the end line, or if there is any other infringement by the attacking team, the defending team shall be awarded the ball on the end line where the play originally started.

Note: If the attacking team was putting the ball in play from a penalty corner, then the defending team would be awarded a free-kick anywhere in the circle.

SEC. 3. If the ball goes out-of-bounds off the feet of two opponents or from the hands of two opponents, the ball shall be tossed up between them at a spot five yards from the side line or end line opposite the spot from where the ball went out. All players must be five yards away from the ball until it has been played. No one may score directly from the toss-up.

Penalty: For an infringement of this rule outside of the circle, a free-kick is awarded on the spot to the opponent. But if the toss-up is taken in the circle, then a penalty corner or free-kick at the edge of the circle would be awarded. (See Rule 9.)

RULE 13--ACCIDENTS AND INTERFERENCE WITH THE GAME

SEC. 1.. When a player is temporarily incapacitated, the Umpire shall suspend the game. When the game is resumed, unless a throw-in, penalty corner, or a free-kick has been awarded, the ball shall be tossed-up on a spot to be chosen by the Umpire in whose half of the ground the player was hurt.

   a. A player should not be considered incapacitated because of being winded.
   b. If the Umpire considers that the progress of the game is being interferred with, she shall have authority to suspend the game temporarily.
   c. A ball touching an Umpire or obstacle is in play unless it goes off the field, or if, in the opinion of the Umpire, it should have gone off the field, in which case, usual rules for out-of-bounds apply.

DIGEST OF SPEED-A-WAY RULES

| SITUATION | PENALTY |

PLAYERS AND EQUIPMENT

1. Speed-a-way is played by two teams of eleven players each, designated as five forwards, three halfbacks, two fullbacks, and one goalkeeper.

2. A team has only 11 players, one of whom is disqualified.

   2. Team may play with less than 11 players although it is not advisable.

3. A player other than the Captain requests time-out.

   3. Legal

4. Player enters the game for the fourth time.

   4. Disqualified. Opposing team shall be given possession of the ball in the manner that play ordinarily would have been resumed. Players are allowed to enter the game only when their team has possession of the ball.

5. Player fails to report to the scorekeeper and to be recognized by the nearest Umpire.

   5. Opposing team is given possession of the ball.

OFFICIALS

1. Officials for a match game shall be two Umpires, four Linesmen, a Timekeeper, and a Scorekeeper.

KICKOFF

1. To start the game, at the beginning of each quarter, and after a score has been made, both teams line-up in their own half of the field; all

   1. The kick-off shall be taken over again by the same player, for the ball is not in play until the whistle is blown.

SITUATION	PENALTY

players except the kicker must be five yards away from the ball. The player in the center takes the kick-off before the Umpire blows her whistle.

2. The player taking the kick-off plays the ball before it has been played by another player.

2. Free-kick for the opponent. All players must be five yards away.

3. A player stands closer than five yards from the ball on the kick-off.

3. If a member of the kicking team makes the infringement, the other team gets the ball on a free-kick; if a member of the non-kicking team commits the infringement, then a free-kick is given the kicking team.

4. A player touches a ground ball with her hands, but her opponent gains possession of the ball and dribbles away from her opponent.

4. The foul is not called, if in the opinion of the Umpire, it would be an advantage to the offending team.

5. Players of both teams line up on own side of the center line, none closer than five yards from the ball other than the player taking the kick-off.

5. Legal. There is no restraining line. Players of both teams may stand on but not over the center line.

6. Player on Team A on a kick-off attempts to lift to a teammate. Player on Team B intercepts and plays it as an aerial ball.

6. Legal, provided that the player did not cross the center line before the ball in the air or after one bounce.

THE GAME

1. The game shall consist of four quarters of eight minutes each with a two minute rest interval between the first and second and the third and fourth quarters, and a ten minute interval between halves.

SITUATION	PENALTY

2. Teams wish to shorten playing time.

2. The periods may be shortened by mutual consent of the captains and the officials.

3. Team A wins the toss.

3. The winner of the toss shall have the option of putting the ball in play or of selecting their goal.

4. A score is made.

4. Team which is scored upon shall have the choice of kicking-off or of letting the opponents kick.

5. Opponent crosses the center line before the ball is kicked but gains no advantage.

5. Play continues.

6. The ball is out-of-bounds wh when time-out is called.

6. Play begins with a throw-in if out at the side-line or if out at the end-line, play begins with a throw-in, drop-kick, punt, or place-kick.

7. Ball is in play when time-out is called for an injury.

7. The ball shall be put in play with a throw-in at the side line nearest the spot where the ball was when time-out was taken. The team who had possession of the ball when time was called puts the ball in play.

8. Time-out is requested following a foul.

8. Play begins with the penalty for the foul.

9. Time-out is requested just after a goal has been scored.

9. Play shall be resumed by a kick-off.

SCORING

1. Field goal is made from within the striking circle.

1. Three points.

2. Field goal is made from outside the striking circle.

2. No score. Out-of-bound rules apply.

3. Defending player accidentally kicks the ball through the goal.

3. Goal counts for the attacking team provided that the attack-

SITUATION	PENALTY
	ing team had kicked the ball while the ball was within the striking circle.
4. Field goal is scored directly from a penalty corner.	4. Goal does not count. The ball is awarded to the opponent at the edge of the striking ircle.
5. A field goal is scored directly from a free-kick	5. Goal does not count.
6. The ball is in the air on the way to a goal or a touchdown when the whistle blows for end of playing time. A score is made.	6. The score does not count. The Timekeeper's whistle indicates the end of playing time.
7. A touchdown is made.	7. Two points.
8. A drop-kick is made under the crossbar.	8. Three points provided the ball is kicked from within the circle.
9. The ball is punted through the goal posts.	9. No score. Out-of-bound rules apply.
10. On the throw-in from the end-line the ball is passed twice for a score.	10. The touchdown does not count. Whenever the ball is thrown in from the end-line or from the side-line between the defending team's 25-yard line and the goal line, there must be three passes before a touchdown may be scored. For an infringement of this rule, the opponent shall be awarded the ball where the play originally started, unless the ball from the end-line has been played as a penalty corner, in which case the defending team would get a free-kick at the edge of the circle.
11. A player runs with the ball between the goal posts.	11. The score does not count. Out-of-bound rules apply.
12. A forward pass is legally intercepted by a defensive player who is behind the goal line.	12. No score. Defensive team gains possession of the ball out-of-bounds.

SITUATION	PENALTY
13. The ball is thrown between the goal posts.	13. No score. Out-of-bound rules apply.
14. A player catches a touch-down pass between the goal posts.	14. No score. Out-of-bound rules apply.
15. A player lifts the ball to herself and runs over the end-line for a touchdown.	15. Legal.
16. A player is in the act of catching a pass over the end-line, and she is deliberately fouled, causing her to lose the ball.	16. Touchdown counts.
17. In order to prevent a field goal, the goalkeeper picks up the ball with her hands.	17. Legal. The goalkeeper is the only player allowed to pick up a ground ball.

TIE BALL

1. Two opposing players catch the ball simultaneously.	1. A toss-up.
2. On the toss-up one of the players taps the ball directly to a teammate over the goal line.	2. The score does not count. Opposing team is awarded a free-kick where play originally started.
3. Player has possession of the ball; opponent places one or both hands on the ball in an attempt to tie the ball.	3. Not legal. Free-kick is awarded the team originally in possession of the ball.

FREE-KICK

1. A foul is called outside the circle.	1. Umpire blows the whistle and indicates who is to take the free-kick and where. (Usually at the spot where the infringement occurred.)
2. A free-kick is awarded	2. A place-kick is taken where the foul was committed. All players except the kicker must be five yards from the ball.

SITUATION	PENALTY
3. Player taking the free-kick plays the ball again before it has been played by another player.	3. Free-kick for opponent.
4. Goal is scored from free-kick.	4. Not legal.
5. Opponents stand closer than five yards on a free-kick. No advantage gained.	5. Play continues.
6. A player picks up a ground ball.	6. Free-kick for the opponent.
7. Player while running with the ball is tagged.	7. Free-kick for the opponent.
8. A player shoves, pushes, charges or strikes her opponent.	8. Free-kick.
9. A player kicks her opponent or dangerously kicks the ball into her opponent.	9. Free-kick.
10. Two players guard a player who is in possession of the ball and who cannot make a successful play.	10. Free-kick for the team who had possession of the ball.
11. The attacking team commits a foul in its opponent's striking circle.	11. Free-kick from any point inside the circle.
12. A player picks up a kicked ball which has bounced more than once.	12. Free-kick for the opponent.
13. A ball is thrown and takes one bounce. It is touched by a player.	13. Free-kick for the opponent.
14. Player has ball trapped under her foot or between the feet. Opponent kicks the ball out.	14. Legal, provided the player making the kick does not have personal contact with the opponent.
15. Ball is lifted to a teammate. Opponent intercepts on the fly.	15. Legal. Ball may also be intercepted and played as an aerial ball on the first bounce.

SITUATION	PENALTY
16. Player drop-kicks the ball. Opponent catches it after one bounce and plays it as an aerial ball.	16. Legal.
17. Ground ball hits the knee of a player. Player plays it as an aerial ball.	17. Not an aerial ball. The ground ball must be touched by the foot to change it to an aerial ball.
18. Player catches the ball on the first bounce after a lift-up or punt. She fumbles it to the ground.	18. The ball can no longer be an aerial ball. It must be touched by the foot to again create an aerial ball.
19. A player to avoid being tagged juggles the ball.	19. Legal.
20. A player after running 10 or 15 feet to catch a juggle, remains in a stationary position.	20. Legal. Player may not be tagged. The player may hold the ball for three seconds.
21. Goalie picks up a ground ball outside the circle.	21. Goalkeeper's privileges are not confined to the circle.
22. A player knocks the ball from her opponent's hand.	22. Free-kick for the team that had possession of the ball.
23. The team taking the kick-off crosses the center line before the ball is kicked.	23. Free-kick for the opponent.
24. A player runs with the ball. She stops and is tagged.	24. Legal tag. Free-kick for the team that did not have the ball.
25. The player taking the free-kick kicks the ball backwards.	25. Legal. The ball may be kicked in any direction.
26. Player on Team A kicks the ball. Player on Team B touches the ball with a hand. The ball touches the ground.	26. Must be played as a ground ball.

PENALTY CORNER

1. A penalty corner is awarded if the defending team commits a foul in its own circle.	1. The wing of the attacking team shall put the ball in play from a point on the goal line 15 yards from the nearer goal

56

SITUATION	PENALTY
	posts (where the circle bisects the end-line) with a throw-in, a punt, a place-kick, or a drop-kick. All players must be five yards away.
2. The defending team commits a foul on the penalty corner play.	2. Penalty corner.
3. There is an infringement of the rule by the attacking team.	3. Free-kick at a point anywhere in the circle by the defending team.
4. A throw-in is used; only two passes are made before a touchdown is scored.	4. Score does not count. Free-kick for the defending team at a point anywhere in the circle.
5. The wing place-kicks the ball to her own player who runs over the end-line for a touchdown.	5. Legal.
6. On a penalty corner the attacking wing lifts the ball to a teammate who immediately throws the ball back to the wing.	6. Legal. Three passes are not necessary.

OUT-OF-BOUNDS

SITUATION	PENALTY
1. Ball goes out-of-bounds over side-line.	1. The ball shall be thrown-in by the opponent of the player who last touched it.
2. The ball is caught after it leaves the thrower's hands.	2. Legal.
3. The opponent enters the alley before the ball has left the thrower's hands.	3. The play is repeated.
4. The ball is sent out-of-bounds over the end-line by the attacking team.	4. The ball is put in play at a point 15 yards from the goal posts on the side that the ball went out, and the ball is awarded to the opponents. All players must be 5 yards from the ball.

SITUATION	PENALTY
5. The attacking team does not have three passes before scoring a touchdown from a throw-in at the end-line.	5. The score does not count. If the play from the end-line was from a penalty corner, then the defending team is given a free-kick at the edge of the circle; if the play was for out-of-bounds, then the opponent puts the ball in play from the end-line.
6. The ball goes off the feet of two opponents and goes out-of-bounds.	6. The ball shall be tossed up between them at a spot five yards from the side-line or end-line opposite the spot from where the ball went out. All players must be five yards away.
7. A player scores directly from the toss-up.	7. Not legal. Free-kick at the spot where play originally started.
8. The ball is sent out-of-bounds over the end-line by the defending team.	8. Whenever the ball is sent out-of-bounds over the end-line by the defending team, or by the attacking team, the ball is put in play with a throw-in, punt, drop-kick, or a place-kick at a point 15 yards from the goal posts on the side that the ball went out.
9. A player puts the ball in play on a throw-in, plays the ball before it has been played by another player.	9. Opponent gets the ball.

SPEED-A-WAY FILM

Demonstrating The Game of Speed-A-Way

FILM CONTENT:

1. The Game
2. Playing Field
3. Composition of Teams
4. Methods of Scoring
5. Making an Aerial Ball
6. Fouls
7. Out-of-Bounds
8. Offensive Play
9. Defensive Play

ONE REEL, SOUND

RENTAL

Color---$3.75 for the First Day   Black and White---$2.50 for the First Day.

For additional rental days, the cost is 1/2 the original price.

SALE

Color---$95.00   Black and White---$50.00

Available From

MARJORIE S. LARSEN

1754 MIDDLEFIELD   STOCKTON 4, CALIFORNIA